HEY, LOOK ME OVER
Cy Coleman's
BROADWAY SHOWSTOPPERS

C000129720

WARNER BROS. PUBLICATIONS - THE GLOBAL LEADER IN PRINT
USA: 15800 NW 48th Avenue, Miami, FL 33014

WARNER/CHAPPELL MUSIC

CANADA: 40 SHEPPARD AVE. WEST, SUITE 800
TORONTO, ONTARIO, M2N 6K9
SCANDINAVIA: P.O. BOX 533, VENDEVAGEN 85 B
S-182 15, DANDERYD, SWEDEN
AUSTRALIA: P.O. BOX 353
3 TALAVERA ROAD, NORTH RYDE N.S.W. 2113

Carisch
NUOVA CARISCH

ITALY: VIA CAMPANIA, 12
20098 S. GIULIANO MILANESE (MI)
ZONA INDUSTRIALE SESTO ULTERIANO
SPAIN: MAGALLANES, 25
28015 MADRID
FRANCE: 20, RUE DE LA VILLE-L'EVEQUE, 75008 PARIS

IMP
INTERNATIONAL MUSIC PUBLICATIONS LIMITED

ENGLAND: SOUTHEND ROAD,
WOODFORD GREEN, ESSEX IG8 8HN
GERMANY: MARSTALLSTR. 8, D-80539 MUNCHEN
DENMARK: DANMUSIK, VOGNMAGERGADE 7
DK 1120 KOBENHAVNK

© 1998 WARNER BROS. PUBLICATIONS
All Rights Reserved

C O N T E N T S

C O N T E N T S

BIG SPENDER
From The Musical "SWEET CHARITY"

Music by
CY COLEMAN

Lyrics by
DOROTHY FIELDS

REAL LIVE GIRL

From The Musical "LITTLE ME"

**Music by
CY COLEMAN**

**Lyrics by
CAROLYN LEIGH**

WITH EVERY BREATH I TAKE

From The Musical "CITY OF ANGELS"

Music by
CY COLEMAN

Lyrics by
DAVID ZIPPEL

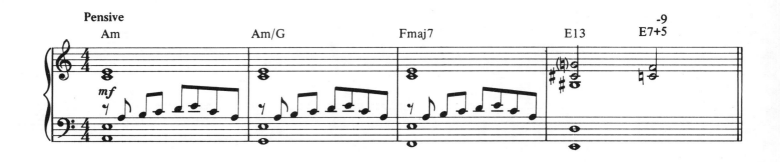

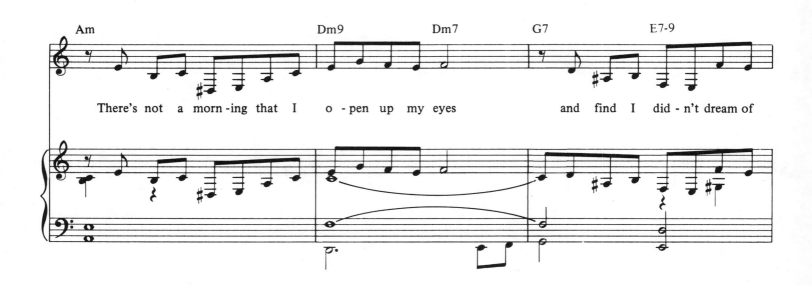

There's not a morn-ing that I o-pen up my eyes   and find I did-n't dream of

you.   With-out a warn-ing, though it's nev-er a sur-prise,   soon as I a-wake

COME FOLLOW THE BAND

From The Musical "BARNUM"

Music by
CY COLEMAN

Lyrics by
MICHAEL STEWART

19

SOUTHERN COMFORT
From The Musical "WELCOME TO THE CLUB"

Music by
CY COLEMAN

Lyrics by
A.E. HOTCHNER and CY COLEMAN

Lyrics:

1. Black-eyed peas, _____ Hon-ey bees, _____
2. Pe-can pies, _____ Sul-try skies, _____
3. Smell of pine, _____ New York wine, _____
4. South-ern Belle, _____ North-ern gent, _____

A la-zy ham-mock swing-in' in the breeze. _____
And sit-tin' on a rock-er swat-tin' flies. _____
When you're a-cross the Mas-on Dix-on line. _____
A com-bin-a-tion that is heav-en sent. _____

NEVER MET A MAN I DIDN'T LIKE

From The Musical "THE WILL ROGERS FOLLIES"

Music by
CY COLEMAN

Lyrics by
BETTY COMDEN and ADOLPH GREEN

OUR PRIVATE WORLD
From The Musical "ON THE TWENTIETH CENTURY"

Music by
CY COLEMAN

Lyrics by
BETTY COMDEN and ADOLPH GREEN

Moderately, with expression

Our Pri - vate World _____ is like a play a - bout a pair of lov - ers. The plot says on - ly we may en - ter and

36

TALL HOPE

From The Musical "WILDCAT"

Music by
CY COLEMAN

Lyrics by
CAROLYN LEIGH

38

IT'S NOT WHERE YOU START
From The Musical "SEESAW"

**Music by
CY COLEMAN**

**Lyrics by
DOROTHY FIELDS**

THE RHYTHM OF LIFE

From The Musical "SWEET CHARITY"

Music by
CY COLEMAN

Lyrics by
DOROTHY FIELDS

FUNNY

From The Musical "CITY OF ANGELS"

Music by
CY COLEMAN

Lyrics by
DAVID ZIPPEL

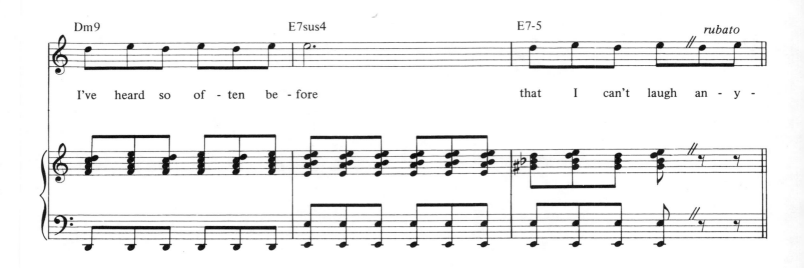

I've heard so of-ten be-fore that I can't laugh an-y-

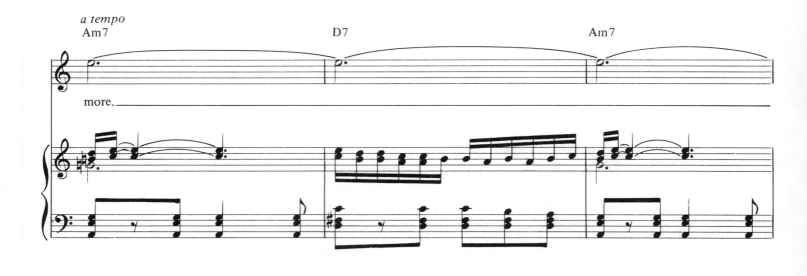

more.

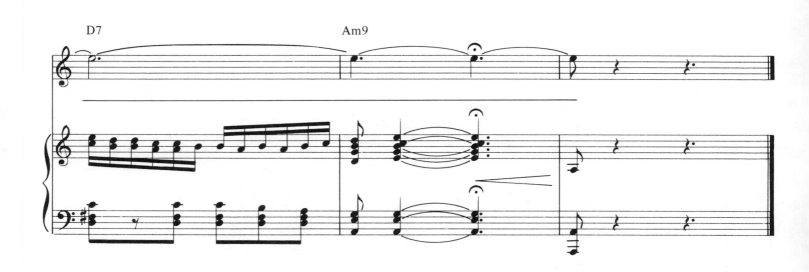

VERONIQUE
From The Musical "ON THE TWENTIETH CENTURY"

Music by
CY COLEMAN

Lyrics by
BETTY COMDEN and ADOLPH GREEN

Ve - ro - nique, she wink an eye, Ve - ro - nique, the
Ve - ro - nique, "Let Bis - marck in." No - tre Dame says,

bul - lets fly, Ve - ro - nique, she close her door and start the Fran - co -
"That's no sin." Em - per - or says, "Please come through and France will make a

Prus - sian War.
saint of you."

Ve - ro - nique, the femme fa - tale,
Ve - ro - nique, up - on its knee,

Ve - ro - nique, the
see the whole a -

fleur de mal,
ca - de - mie.

Ve - ro - nique, shut Bis - marck out and make the pop - u -
Ve - ro - nique, é - cou - tes toi the French in - tel - li -

la - tion shout: "Save our cit - y,
gen - si - a. And her pa - pa say,

let old Bis - marck
"Do it for your

have a look, Save our Par - is,
coun - try's sake." And her ma - ma say,

you'll look good in
"Do it and I

Ve-ro-nique, Ve-ro-nique, Ve-ro-nique, Ve-ro-nique, Ve-ro-nique, Ve-ro-nique.

Ve-ro-nique, she face the Hun, Ve-ro-nique, she face the gun,

Ve-ro-nique, she start to dance while shout-ing brave-ly, "Vive la France!"

Ve-ro-nique, a sud-den hush. Ve-ro-nique, shout, "Kill the Boche!"

sud - den - ly   a   shot, then two, and   she   fall life - less dans la rue.

Slowly and gradually faster

But   her   spir - it   danc - es   on a - bove the fray,

cresc. poco a poco

p

Li - ber - té,   e - ga - li - té, fra - ter - ni - té.

France is   saved   and   free - dom once a - gain can speak,

mf

YOU'RE NOTHING WITHOUT ME

From The Musical "CITY OF ANGELS"

Music by
CY COLEMAN

Lyrics by
DAVID ZIPPEL

You are some gum - shoe, you just don't think_ well.
You are so jeal - ous of my track rec - ord.

Get this dumb gum - shoe, you come_ from my ink - well.
Tol - stoy, do tell_ us, your fee - ble hack rec - ord.

66

68

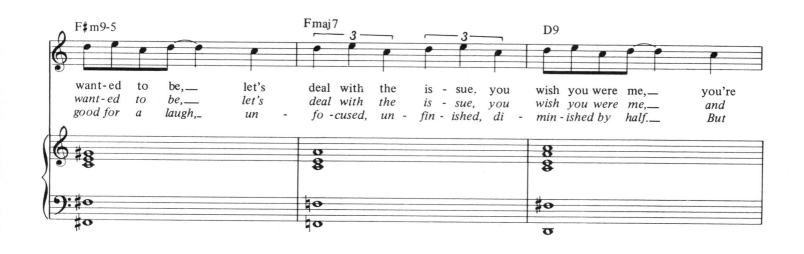

F#m9-5 ... Fmaj7 ... D9

want-ed to be,— let's deal with the is-sue, you wish you were me,— you're
want-ed to be,— let's deal with the is-sue, you wish you were me,— and
good for a laugh,— un-fo-cused, un-fin-ished, di-min-ished by half.— But

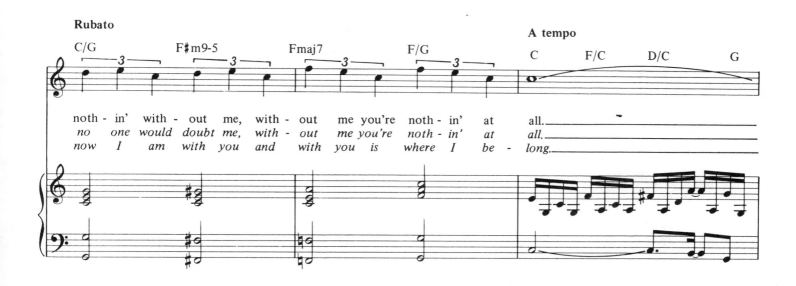

Rubato

A tempo

C/G ... F#m9-5 ... Fmaj7 ... F/G ... C F/C D/C G

noth-in' with-out me, with-out me you're noth-in' at all._____
no one would doubt me, with-out me you're noth-in' at all._____
now I am with you and with you is where I be-long._____

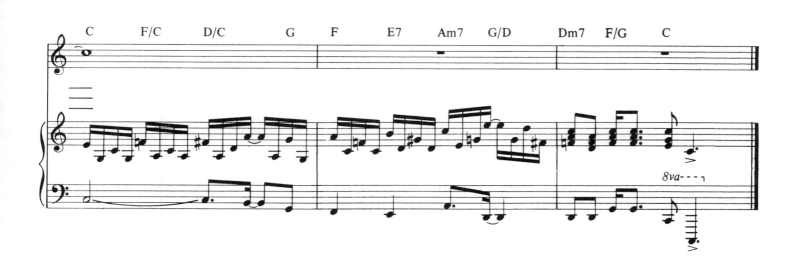

C F/C D/C G F E7 Am7 G/D Dm7 F/G C

8va----

POOR EVERYBODY ELSE
From The Musical "SEESAW"

Music by
CY COLEMAN

Lyrics by
DOROTHY FIELDS

EV'RYBODY TODAY IS TURNING ON

From The Musical "I LOVE MY WIFE"

Music by
CY COLEMAN

Lyrics by
MICHAEL STEWART

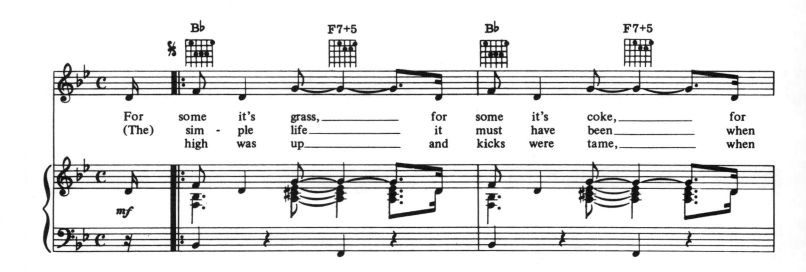

PIECE OF CAKE
From The Musical "WELCOME TO THE CLUB"

Music by
CY COLEMAN

Lyrics by
A.E. HOTCHNER
and CY COLEMAN

THE COLORS OF MY LIFE
From The Musical "BARNUM"

Music by
CY COLEMAN

Lyrics by
MICHAEL STEWART

IF MY FRIENDS COULD SEE ME NOW

From The Musical "SWEET CHARITY"

Music by
CY COLEMAN

Lyrics by
DOROTHY FIELDS

91

SHE'S A NUT
From The Musical "ON THE TWENTIETH CENTURY"

Music by
CY COLEMAN

Lyrics by
BETTY COMDEN and ADOLPH GREEN

93

104

HEY, LOOK ME OVER
From The Musical "WILDCAT"

Music by
CY COLEMAN

Lyrics by
CAROLYN LEIGH

Interlude *(ad lib.)*

No - bod - y in the world was ev - er with - out a pray'r;

How can you win the world, if no - bod - y knows you're there.

Kid, when you need the crowd, the tick - ets are hard to sell;

Still you can lead the crowd, if you can get up and yell:

LOST AND FOUND
From The Musical "CITY OF ANGELS"

Music by
CY COLEMAN

Lyrics by
DAVID ZIPPEL

109

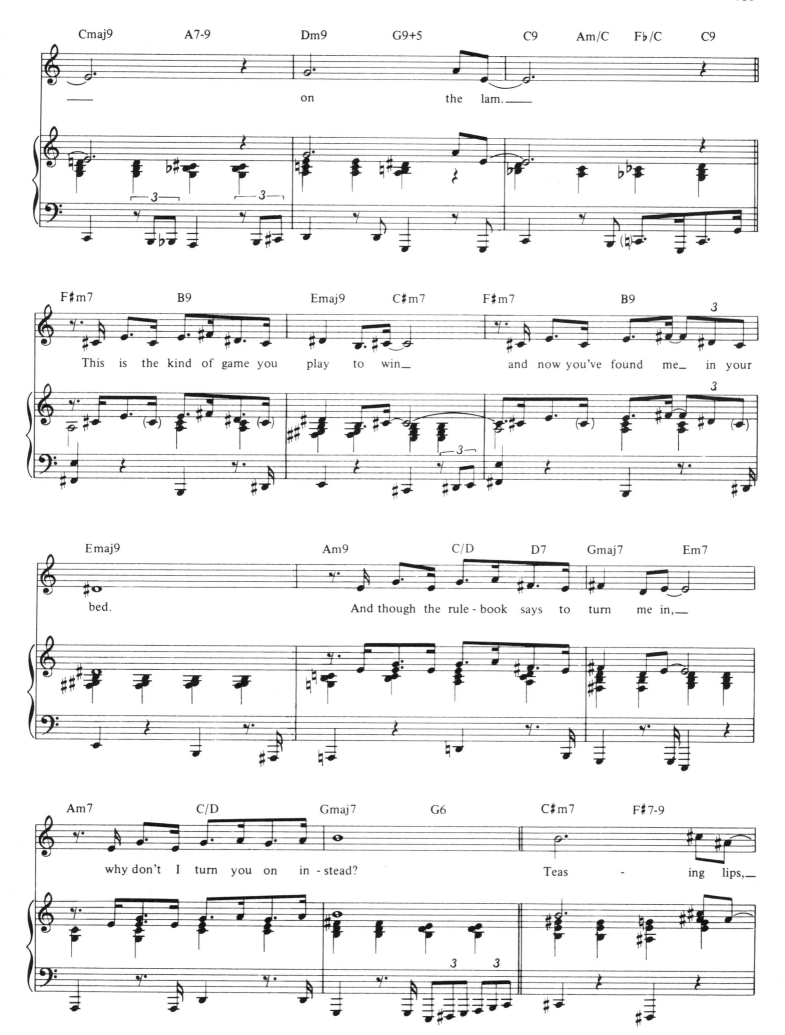

110

RIO
From The Musical "WELCOME TO THE CLUB"

Music by
CY COLEMAN

Lyrics by
A.E. HOTCHNER
and CY COLEMAN

Moderate Latin Beat

Meltzer
I'm gon-na

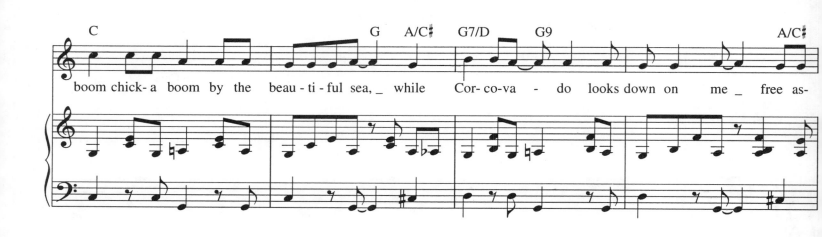

boom chick-a boom by the beau-ti-ful sea, _ while Cor-co-va-do looks down on me _ free as-

so-ci-at-in' in Por-tu-gee, _ I'm gon-na be in Ri-o. _____ Where

114

119

BIGGER ISN'T BETTER

From The Musical "BARNUM"

Music by
CY COLEMAN

Lyrics by
MICHAEL STEWART

124

NO MAN LEFT FOR ME
From The Musical "THE WILL ROGERS FOLLIES"

Music by
CY COLEMAN

Lyrics by
BETTY COMDEN and ADOLPH GREEN

128

130

ev - 'ry time I start_ this feel - ing floods my heart,_ he needs me to feed the cat:_

_ Tho' when I'm by my - self I'm so lone - some,

a par - ty makes it twice as grim._____ The peo - ple joke and play my

mind is miles a - way,-- It's off on the road with him. ___

D.S. al Coda

THERE IS A SUCKER BORN EV'RY MINUTE

From The Musical "BARNUM"

Music by
CY COLEMAN

Lyrics by
MICHAEL STEWART

1. There is a suck-er _____ born ev-'ry min-ute, _____
2. Each bless-ed hour _____ brings six-ty of 'em _____
3. There is a suck-er _____ born ev-'ry min-ute, _____

SOMEONE WONDERFUL I MISSED
From The Musical "I LOVE MY WIFE"

Music by
CY COLEMAN

Lyrics by
MICHAEL STEWART

THERE'S GOTTA BE SOMETHING
BETTER THAN THIS

From The Musical "SWEET CHARITY"

Music by
CY COLEMAN

Lyrics by
DOROTHY FIELDS

WHAT TAKES MY FANCY
From The Musical "WILDCAT"

Music by
CY COLEMAN

Lyrics by
CAROLYN LEIGH

150

DEEP DOWN INSIDE

From The Musical "LITTLE ME"

Music by
CY COLEMAN

Lyrics by
CAROLYN LEIGH

Some-where,   though you think he fell   a - sleep down   in - side,
Some-times   got - ta take that broom 'n' sweep down   in - side,

Deep down dig - a, dig - a,}
Sweep down dig - a, dig - a,} DEEP DOWN IN - SIDE.

Interlude I

In e - ven the worst of var - mints,

you'll find a good deed,   Down un - der the out - er gar - ments

LOOK AROUND
From The Musical "THE WILL ROGERS FOLLIES"

Music by
CY COLEMAN

Lyrics by
BETTY COMDEN and ADOLPH GREEN

158

THE TENNIS SONG
From The Musical "CITY OF ANGELS"

**Music by
CY COLEMAN**

**Lyrics by
DAVID ZIPPEL**

164

NOBODY DOES IT LIKE ME

From The Musical "SEESAW"

Music by
CY COLEMAN

Lyrics by
DOROTHY FIELDS

YOU CAN ALWAYS COUNT ON ME

From The Musical "CITY OF ANGELS"

Music by
CY COLEMAN

Lyrics by
DAVID ZIPPEL

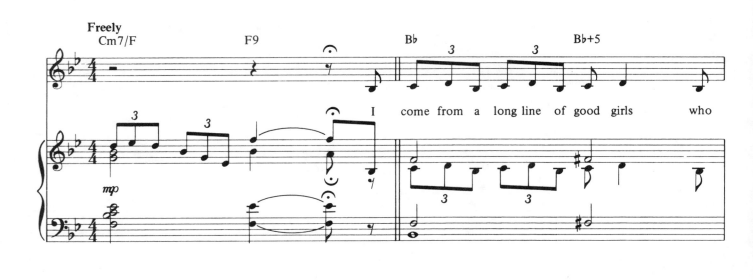

I come from a long line of good girls who

choose the wrong guy to be sweet on; the girl with a face that says "wel - come" that

men can wipe their feet on. I'm there when he calls me, the trust - ed girl Fri - day, al -

right, but what good does it do me a-lone on a Sat-ur-day night?

I don't need a map, I nat-'ral-ly head for the dead end street.
mat-ter of fact, if you want an ill-fat-ed love af-fair,
my kind of dame no doubt will die out like the di-no-saurs,

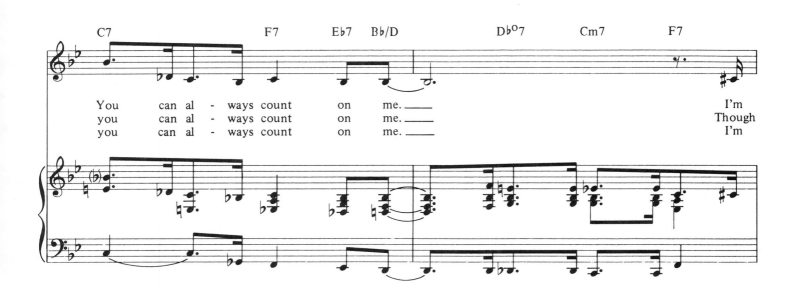

You can al-ways count on me. I'm
you can al-ways count on me. Though
you can al-ways count on me. I'm

caught in a trap; when joy is ap-proach-ing then I re - treat.__ I'm at home with mis - er - y.
I've made a pact to car - ry out re - search be - fore I care,__ men don't give a war - ran - ty.
sole - ly to blame, my head gives ad - vice that my heart ig - nores.__ I'm my on - ly en - e - my.__

__ I've been the "oth - er wo - man"since my pu - ber - ty be - gan,__ I
__ One Joe who swore he's sin - gle got me sort - a crocked,the beast;__ I
__ I choose the kind who can - not in - tro - duce the girl he's with;__ they're

crashed the jun - ior prom and met the on - ly__ mar - ried man.__ I'm
woke up on - ly slight - ly shocked that I'd de - frocked a priest.__ Or
lots of smirk - ing mo - tel clerks who call me __ Miss - us Smith,__ but

FAVORITE SON

From The Musical "THE WILL ROGERS FOLLIES"

Music by
CY COLEMAN

Lyrics by
BETTY COMDEN and ADOLPH GREEN

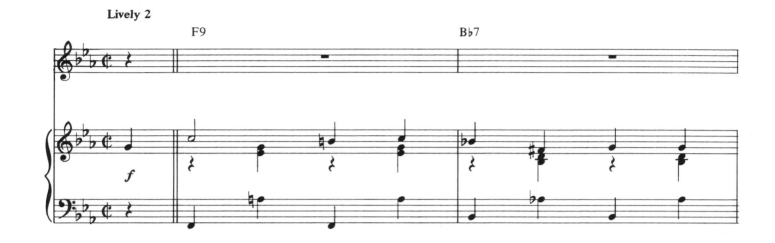

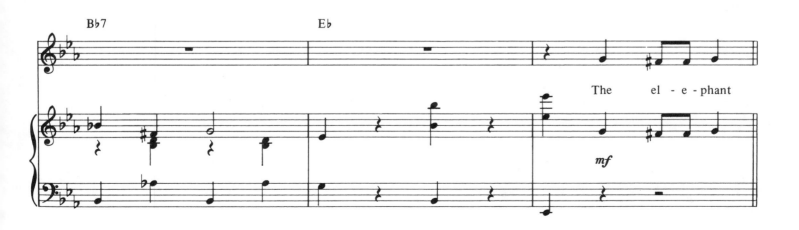

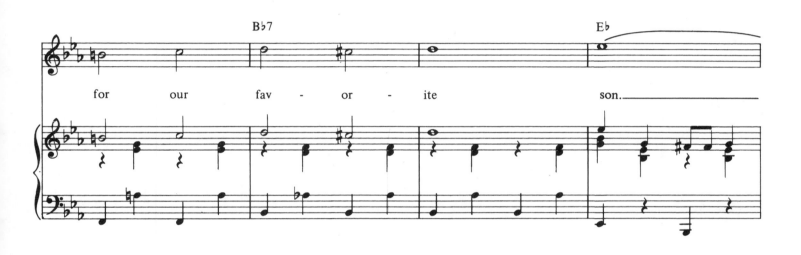

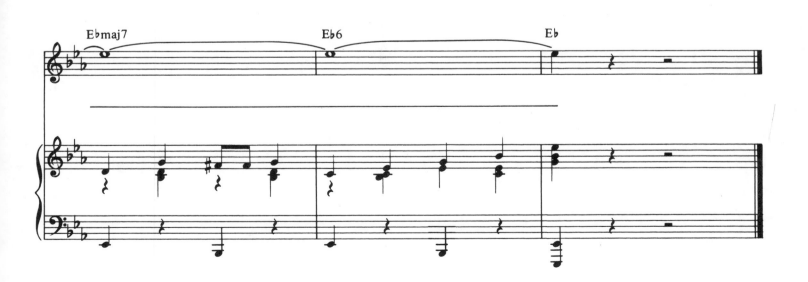

I'VE GOT YOUR NUMBER

From The Musical "LITTLE ME"

Music by
CY COLEMAN

Lyrics by
CAROLYN LEIGH

Refrain

187

HEY THERE, GOOD TIMES

From The Musical "I LOVE MY WIFE"

Music by
CY COLEMAN

Lyrics by
MICHAEL STEWART

Moderately, with a lift

Bb 6

Hey There Good Times, here I am.___ Wel - come back your ba - by lamb.___
Hey There Good Times, let me in.___ Ask me how the hell I been.___